EYEWITNESS
EAGLE &
BIRDS OF PREY

Kestrel skeleton

White-bellied sea eagle

Verreaux's eagle

European
kestrel

EYEWITNESS
EAGLE &
BIRDS OF PREY

Common,
or crested,
caracara

Written by
JEMIMA PARRY-JONES
The National Birds of Prey Centre

Photographed by
FRANK GREENAWAY

Saker falcon

Bald eagle

DK

African
hawk eagle

Peregrine
falcon

Foot of
wedgetailed
eagle

Egyptian
vulture

African harrier
hawk

White-backed
vulture

Penguin
Random
House

Project editor David Pickering
Art editor Kati Poynor
Assistant editor Julie Ferris
Managing editor Gill Denton
Managing art editor Julia Harris
Production Charlotte Traill
Picture research Rachel Leach
DTP designer Nicola Studdart
Consultant Colin Shawyer

RELAUNCH EDITION

DK UK
Senior editor Francesca Baines
Senior art editor Spencer Holbrook
US senior editor Margaret Parrish
Jacket coordinator Claire Gell
Jacket designer Natalie Godwin
Jacket design development manager Sophia MTT
Producer, pre-production Jacqueline Street
Producer Vivienne Yong
Managing art editor Philip Letsu
Publisher Andrew Macintyre
Associate publishing director Liz Wheeler
Design director Stuart Jackman
Publishing director Jonathan Metcalf

DK INDIA
Editorial team Bharti Bedi, Ateendriya Gupta
Design team Nidhi Rastogi, Tanvi Sahu
DTP designer Pawan Kumar
Senior DTP designer Harish Aggarwal
Picture researcher Sakshi Saluja
Jacket designer Dhirendra Singh
Managing jackets editor Saloni Singh
Pre-production manager Balwant Singh
Managing editor Kingshuk Ghoshal
Managing art editor Govind Mittal

First American Edition, 1997
This edition published in the United States in 2016 by
DK Publishing, 345 Hudson Street, New York, New York 10014

Copyright © 1997, 2016 Dorling Kindersley Limited
DK, a Division of Penguin Random House LLC

16 17 18 19 20 10 9 8 7 6 5 4 3 2 1
001—294905—June/16

Published in Great Britain by Dorling Kindersley Limited.

A catalog record for this book is available from the Library of Congress.

ISBN: 978-1-4654-5172-9 (Paperback)
ISBN: 978-1-4654-5173-6 (ALB)

DK books are available at special discounts when purchased in bulk for
sales promotions, premiums, fund-raising, or educational use. For details, contact:
DK Publishing Special Markets, 345 Hudson Street, New York, New York 10014
SpecialSales@dk.com

Printed and bound in China

A WORLD OF IDEAS:
SEE ALL THERE IS TO KNOW
www.dk.com

Contents

Tawny eagle

What is a bird of prey?

Birds of prey are not the only birds that hunt for their food, nor the only birds that eat meat, have hooked beaks, or fly very well, but they are the only birds that have all these characteristics. They also have one very distinctive feature: they kill with their feet. Most are called raptors, from the Latin *raptare*, meaning "to seize," because they seize their prey with their feet.

Special diet
Some raptors will eat almost anything; others are specialists. One of the most specialized is the snail kite of Florida. It lives on a diet of water snails.

Primary feathers are fanned out for landing

Tail used for steering, soaring, and braking

A vulture's powerful beak rips open carcasses of large animals

Vultures have weak feet because they don't need to kill their prey

Catch it when it's dead
Vultures are the major exception to the rule that birds of prey hunt their food. Vultures are specialized in scavenging—finding dead animals. Most will spend much of their time soaring high in the sky, scanning a wide area for carrion (dead flesh).

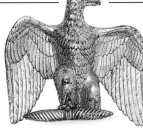

Symbol and standard

Raptors have been used for centuries as symbols for gods or as emblems for armies. This eagle standard (above) comes from the French army, c.1800.

Ravens eat meat in much the same way as many birds of prey

Carnivorous birds

Many meat-eating birds are not birds of prey. For example, magpies hunt and kill small birds. Ravens such as these (above), which belong to the crow family, have a similar diet to that of buzzards. They have strong, pointed beaks with which they kill young rabbits, and even the occasional lamb. But only raptors kill with their feet.

Wing feathers fan out to give extra lift

Born to kill

The tawny eagle (left) is a perfect hunter. It is a superb flier, has lethal raptor feet, and a curved beak that can tear through prey. However, its skill as a hunter can work against it. If the environment is polluted, every animal it eats contains a tiny amount of pollutant, and they end up taking in a large amount.

Female merlins are usually one-third heavier than males; this is average for falcons

In some birds of prey, the male is much more colorful than the female

Does size matter?

Female birds of prey are usually bigger than the males. In sparrowhawks, the female is twice the size of the male. Vultures are one of the exceptions: males and females are usually the same size.

Powerful feet with large curved talons for grasping prey

Eggs and nests

When the breeding season starts, male birds try to gain the affection of a female: they perform display flights and bring food. Once a bond is formed, the new pair builds a nest. The smallest birds of prey brood (sit on) their eggs for 28 days before they hatch; the largest for 54 days. Usually, the females brood the eggs. The males bring food until the chicks are big enough to be left alone safely.

Bald eagle egg

Ural owl egg

Peregrine falcon egg

African pygmy falcon egg

All sorts and sizes

The above eggs (shown actual size) illustrate the variety of raptor eggs. Condors and large vultures lay one egg, most eagles two or three, small birds, like kestrels, about six. A few species, such as snowy owls, lay up to 14.

Starting a family

Males and females usually build their nest together. Male goshawks, however, build three or four nests, by themselves, for females to choose from. Nests are often built in a safe, high place. Only a few raptors, such as harriers and caracaras, build their nests on the ground.

Buzzard eggs in nest

Only the strong survive

Some eagles have two chicks, but if food runs short, the older kills the younger. In a few eagle species, the older always kills the younger. The chicks of smaller raptors do not usually attack each other, but the weakest often dies.

In Verreaux's eagles, the first chick hatched always kills the second, even if there is plenty of food for both

Larger branches are lodged in treetrunk first, then twigs, then leaves

Biggest builder

Bald eagles (right) return to the same nests each year and add to them. One nest in Florida was 9½ ft (2.9 m) wide and 20 ft (6 m) deep.

Who'd be a parent?

For ospreys (left), the breeding cycle lasts about nine months. This is about average. Most raptors breed every year; a few very large birds only breed every other year.

Life support

Embryos develop inside a protective membrane within the egg. As they do so, an air sac appears at the top, or blunt, end of the egg (right).

Air sac

This goshawk egg is blue-green on the inside

1 First crack or "pip" in egg

2 Baby makes one huge push to get out of egg

3 Newly hatched babies rest before feeding

Baby barn owl breaks out

When an egg is ready to hatch, the chick makes a hole in the shell with a pointed lump on top of its beak called an "egg tooth." It keeps tapping—a process that can take up to three days—until it breaks out.

Secondhand nest

These kestrel chicks are in a buzzard nest. Owls, falcons, and New World vultures do not build their own nests. They take over old nests or dig a scrape in a cave, on a cliff ledge, in an old barn, or even on the ledge of a skyscraper. Owls may nest in the hollow of a tree.

Growth of the young raptor

Young birds of prey grow very fast. For their first few weeks they just eat, sleep, and grow. Young sparrowhawks are fully grown and flying after 26 days, and can hunt well enough to feed themselves four weeks later. Larger birds develop more slowly, but even a golden eagle is fledged at two-and-a-half months and is independent three months later.

Two-day-old black vulture chick

10 weeks

2 weeks

3 weeks

6 weeks

8 weeks

1 At two weeks old, this barn owl chick is eight times heavier than it was at hatching. It now weighs 3.5 oz (100 g).

2 The chick can nearly stand up. It is covered in thicker down and can keep warm without its mother.

3 The feathers and facial disk are starting to appear.

4 Nearly fully feathered, it jumps and flaps its wings to strengthen its muscles.

5 It is now fully grown and learning to hunt. In a few weeks it will be able to feed itself.

Unlike many birds, raptor chicks (except owls) have some vision at birth and can take meat from their mother's beak

Egg tooth

Chicks beg for food, cheeping and raising opened mouths to their parents

1 2-day-old peregrine
At two days, all young birds of prey rely on the warmth of their mothers to survive. They eat meat from day one, fed to them in small pieces by their parents.

2 12-day-old peregrine
At 12 days, peregrines start to get a thick white down and can keep themselves warm without the heat from their mother. She can now hunt with the male.

Down inadequate to keep chick warm

Juveniles stay near the nest while their parents still feed them

Juvenile coloration often has a buff edging

3 7-week-old peregrine
This seven-week-old peregrine is nearly fully grown. Once it has fledged it will be called a juvenile, until it gets its adult plumage.

4 Juvenile peregrine
Juveniles hunt in the territory of adult breeding pairs. The adults leave them alone because they are no threat, until they become adults and are ready to breed.

Adults lose the buff edging to the body feathers and become all gray on the shoulders

Young peregrines usually have vertical bars or stripes

Horizontal bars and stripes replace the vertical ones of youth

Beak is strong enough to tear meat after a few weeks

5 Adult peregrine
Some birds, such as kestrels, breed before they are one year old. Others, such as peregrines, start at three or four. Very large birds may not breed until they are six or seven years old.

Characteristic owl ear hole: a long, thin slit

What an earful
Owls have bigger ears than other raptors, as seen in this two-day-old owl chick (above). Like most raptors, they rip up food for chicks. A few birds of prey, such as vultures and snake eagles, regurgitate food.

Feet very soft and weak at this stage; chicks spend their first few weeks sitting on their ankles

How raptors fly

Raptors' wings provide both the power to go forward and the "lift" to stay in the air. As birds flap their wings, the inner part provides most of the lift, the outer part most of the power. Flight feathers improve the airflow over the wings; the tail is used for steering and for braking. The feathers fan out for a fast turn and open out completely as the bird slows to a stop. Most species of raptor have a different wing-shape, which helps the species fly in a way that is suited to the terrain in which they live.

The rounder wing of the true hawk

Sparrowhawk

Forest flying
The hawk family have long tails, which help them turn fast and stop quickly. Their short, rounded wings allow them to take off quickly. This is vital to enable them to catch prey in the wooded areas in which they live.

The primary feathers raised in takeoff position

The tail is raised to help with getting airborne

Powerful legs help to thrust the bird forward and upward

The power comes from the breast muscles

Legs take a while to be drawn up out of the way

Tail closed when bird is flying in a straight line, but opened and tilted when turning

King of the falcons
The arctic gyrfalcon is the largest and fastest of all the falcons. Falcons have long, pointed wings that are not good for soaring or gliding, but are perfect for fast flying. The narrowness of the wing makes them less able to maneuver well. As a result, they are more suited to hunting in open country than in woodland.

Pointed wings

Just hanging around

Eagles, such as this black eagle, are designed for soaring. They are not able to keep up flapping flight for long, and use warm air currents called "thermals" to lift them up, sometimes thousands of feet high, as they watch for prey.

Tail fans out to increase lift when bird is soaring

Outer primaries have to be very flexible

Inner primaries bearing the load

The covert feathers protect the bone, which is very close to the surface of the wing

The alula (see below) fits in here when not in use

Alula is raised when bird is slowing to a stop

Tawny eagle takeoff

During takeoff, a bird's wings are raised first and the legs push the bird off in a jump. As the bird jumps, the first downbeat happens. It is called the power stroke: the wings move forward and downward, giving the bird lift and forward motion.

Lazy flyer

Condors' wings are long and wide, so the birds can soar for hours on rising air currents, looking for dead animals. But they cannot take off easily if full of food, or if they are somewhere flat. In their mountain homes, however, they simply open their wings as they take off from ledges and the updrafts do the rest.

Large wing area enables condor to glide on air currents rather than use the more tiring flapping flight

Large birds also use the legs and feet as air brakes

Braking alula

This red-tailed hawk is in the landing position: its body is almost vertical to the ground. The wing and tail feathers fan out to slow the bird down. At the top of the wings two thumbs, called "alulas," are standing up. All birds have them. They smooth out the airflow above the wings at low speeds, and prevent the birds from stalling.

Styles of flight

All raptors have one of three basic wing shapes. Falcons have slim, pointed wings, suited to sustained high-speed flight. Hawks, forest eagles, and other forest birds have short, rounded wings, which enable them to take off quickly and accelerate rapidly, but make fast, sustained flight too tiring. Vultures and other large raptors have long, rounded wings. These enable them to soar easily on rising air, but cannot be flapped as quickly as the shorter wings of hawks and falcons, which means they are not as fast or as agile.

Diving down to link toes

Once the feet are grasped the birds tumble toward the ground

Bald eagle will turn upside down to meet the other bird's feet

Grasp your partner by the claw

Some birds have very spectacular mating flights. Bald eagles fly really high, grab the feet of their new mate-to-be, spiral downward together, and then release one another. It is thought they also do this to drive off unwanted eagles from the new pair's territory.

Wings stretched back, moving the bird directly upward

After pushing the caracara upward, the legs dangle a little untidily

Vertical takeoff

Caracaras are related to the falcons, but don't have their fast flight. They are much more agile, however. They can even fly vertically off the ground for several feet. This may be to catch insects they disturb while scratching through rotten wood.

Thermals do not form over water, so most raptors avoid flying over large expanses of water

Birds circle ridges to pick up a thermal

Bird reaches the top of thermal, which stops at a certain height

Raptors often glide from thermal to thermal

Upwardly mobile bird of prey

Thermals are the most important aids for soaring birds. A thermal is a column of warm, rising air that forms as the ground heats up during the day. Raptors can rise effortlessly in thermals, which are vital for migration, as well as for soaring, because they save the birds so much energy.

Wings beating fast, tail starting to fan out as the bird starts to hover

Kestrels have very flexible necks that keep their heads still, although their bodies move slightly

The primaries take the strain

Wing out in the upward climb

Helicopter bird

Kestrels hover as they hunt. They use the wind to assist them, flying slowly into it so that their speed and the wind's speed cancel each other out. Hovering enables them to stay still and look out for prey over open country.

Model of a flying machine invented by Leonardo Da Vinci

Roller-coaster life

Raptors looking for a mate often do a beautiful undulating flight to impress prospective partners. They fly high, fold their wings and drop like a stone, open the wings, pulling out of the dive, climb, then close them again in another dive.

Impossible dream

People have always longed to fly like birds but, even if we could make birdlike wings for ourselves, human muscles are far too weak for fligh. According to one estimate, we would have to have chest muscles 6½ ft (2 m) deep if we wanted to fly.

Some kestrels, such as this European kestrel, have longer tails for their size than other falcons

Head thrust forward in landing position

Primaries splayed out and tilted for landing

Wider secondaries still providing enough lift to stay airborne

Landing gear ready for approach

Tawny landing

When they land from above a perch, birds put on the brakes: they fan their tails wide open, throw their legs forward, and raise their feet. Their wings act as brakes and their heads drop so they can see where they are landing.

The center two tail feathers, are called "deck" feathers

Wings and feathers

Feathers allow the bird to fly and keep it warm. A bird has a variety of feathers. Most are contour feathers. The larger ones in the wings and tail are flight feathers. Underneath are down feathers, which keep the bird warm. Then there are specialized feathers: filoplumes act like eyelashes; semiplumes like a cat's whiskers; and bristles help with preening.

Buzzard (rear view)

Zip up your feathers
Feathers have a central shaft with a vane on each side. The vanes are made up of hundreds of tiny barbs (branches) that hook onto each other like a zipper to create the feather's surface.

Growing wing feathers (left) and tail feathers (right) of young gabar goshawk

When fully grown, feathers are dead, like human hair

Primary feathers

Primary wing covers

Feather muscle

Feather develops

Emerging feather

Protective sheath

Central shaft of feather

Vane made of tiny barbs

Quill

If part of the feather under the skin is damaged as it grows, it may remain damaged

How feathers grow
Feathers grow under the skin. They are alive, full of blood, and protected by a sheath as they grow. As the feather emerges, the sheath splits and the feather unfurls.

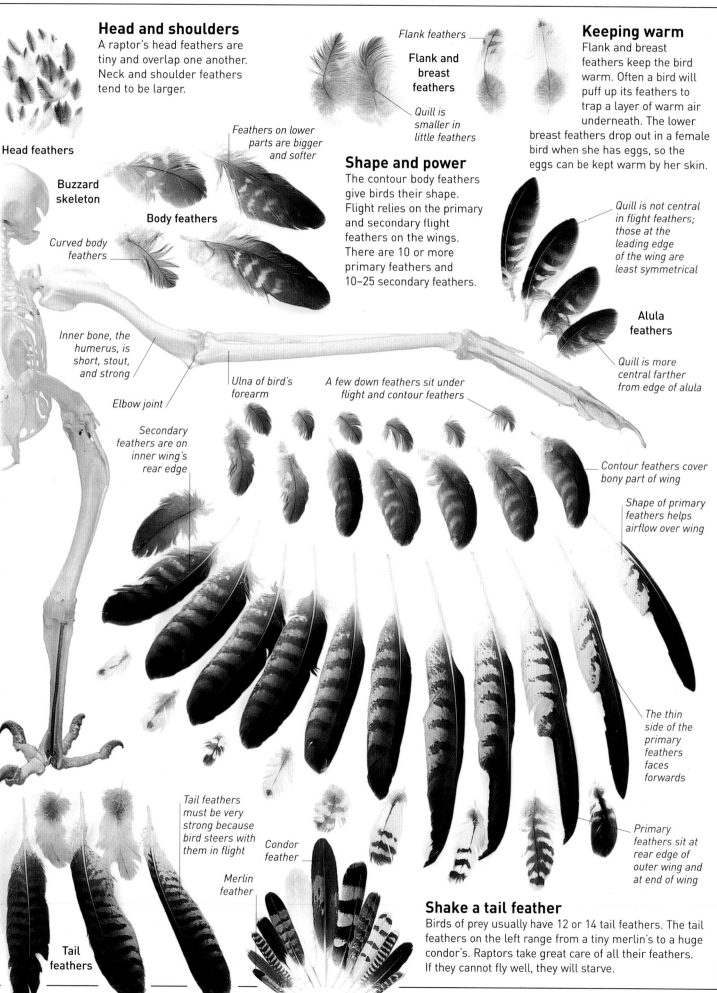

Head and shoulders
A raptor's head feathers are tiny and overlap one another. Neck and shoulder feathers tend to be larger.

Head feathers

Buzzard skeleton

Feathers on lower parts are bigger and softer

Body feathers

Curved body feathers

Flank feathers

Flank and breast feathers

Quill is smaller in little feathers

Shape and power
The contour body feathers give birds their shape. Flight relies on the primary and secondary flight feathers on the wings. There are 10 or more primary feathers and 10–25 secondary feathers.

Keeping warm
Flank and breast feathers keep the bird warm. Often a bird will puff up its feathers to trap a layer of warm air underneath. The lower breast feathers drop out in a female bird when she has eggs, so the eggs can be kept warm by her skin.

Quill is not central in flight feathers; those at the leading edge of the wing are least symmetrical

Alula feathers

Quill is more central farther from edge of alula

Inner bone, the humerus, is short, stout, and strong

Elbow joint

Ulna of bird's forearm

A few down feathers sit under flight and contour feathers

Contour feathers cover bony part of wing

Secondary feathers are on inner wing's rear edge

Shape of primary feathers helps airflow over wing

The thin side of the primary feathers faces forwards

Tail feathers must be very strong because bird steers with them in flight

Condor feather

Merlin feather

Primary feathers sit at rear edge of outer wing and at end of wing

Tail feathers

Shake a tail feather
Birds of prey usually have 12 or 14 tail feathers. The tail feathers on the left range from a tiny merlin's to a huge condor's. Raptors take great care of all their feathers. If they cannot fly well, they will starve.

Inside a bird of prey

Raptors have powerful muscles underneath the feathers. Under the muscles is the skeleton. Protected within the skeleton are the internal organs, which enable the bird to breathe, to breed, and to draw out the nutrition from its food. Birds have an incredibly efficient respiratory system, and their digestive organs are capable of dissolving fur, feathers, small bones, and whole insects.

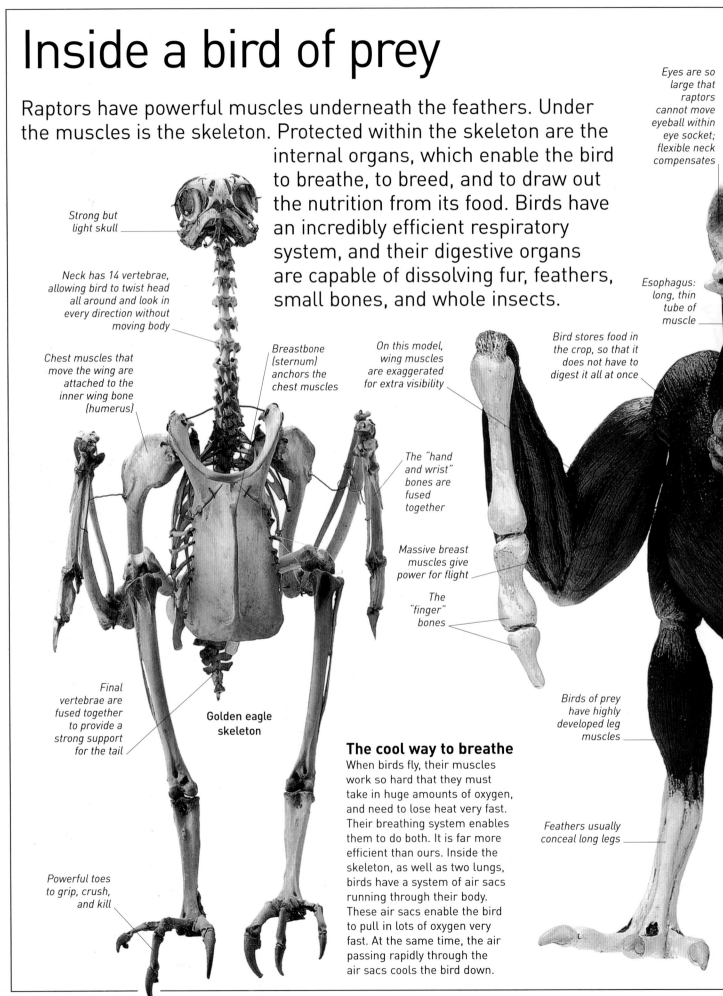

Eyes are so large that raptors cannot move eyeball within eye socket; flexible neck compensates

Strong but light skull

Neck has 14 vertebrae, allowing bird to twist head all around and look in every direction without moving body

Chest muscles that move the wing are attached to the inner wing bone (humerus)

Breastbone (sternum) anchors the chest muscles

On this model, wing muscles are exaggerated for extra visibility

Esophagus: long, thin tube of muscle

Bird stores food in the crop, so that it does not have to digest it all at once

The "hand and wrist" bones are fused together

Massive breast muscles give power for flight

The "finger" bones

Final vertebrae are fused together to provide a strong support for the tail

Golden eagle skeleton

Birds of prey have highly developed leg muscles

Powerful toes to grip, crush, and kill

Feathers usually conceal long legs

The cool way to breathe

When birds fly, their muscles work so hard that they must take in huge amounts of oxygen, and need to lose heat very fast. Their breathing system enables them to do both. It is far more efficient than ours. Inside the skeleton, as well as two lungs, birds have a system of air sacs running through their body. These air sacs enable the bird to pull in lots of oxygen very fast. At the same time, the air passing rapidly through the air sacs cools the bird down.

Bones of spine are largely fused

Weight is concentrated around center

Posture of model is slightly unnatural

Side view of golden eagle's muscles

All birds of prey produce pellets of undigested material, such as this (right). Scientists use these pellets to find out what the bird has been eating. Owl pellets are the most revealing, because an owl's stomachs is less good at digesting small bones.

Falcons and other day-flying raptors digest most of their prey's small bones

Falcon pellet

Digestion time

When birds of prey eat, the meat goes into the crop first, except in owls, which do not have a crop. Then it goes into the stomach, where the unwanted parts are packed into a ball to be regurgitated.

Golden eagle model showing muscles (left)

Golden eagle (right)

The ultimate chest

Muscles make up nearly half the bird of prey's weight. The breast muscles are the largest. They do the work of making the bird fly. Because the big flight muscles are all in the chest, the weight of the bird is kept central, making it more stable in the air. The leg muscles are also very powerful, to grip and crush quarry.

Feet and talons

A raptor's most important tools are its feet. Their size, shape, and strength show what it is capable of catching. For example, kites are large birds, about the size of a small eagle, but their tiny feet only allow them to catch small animals. The peregrine, on the other hand, is smaller than the kite, but has enormous feet and can catch birds almost its own size.

Talons and toes
Talons can be huge on large eagles. In some female eagles, the inner and back talons can be as long as your thumb.

Feathers are fanned out for landing

This bone is the foot bone, although it appears to be part of the leg

A golden eagle's foot
Birds walk on their toes. The bird "foot" has become an extension of the leg. It helps absorb the shock of landing and to push up when taking off.

These bones are the toes, and the talons are the toenails

Falcons' feet are large, but not very strong

Saker falcon foot
Falcons often strike their prey at high speed, so the force of the impact disables, or kills, the prey. Sometimes, they close the foot into a fist and punch the quarry.

Black eagle
The African black eagle has enormous feet and can catch the rock hyrax. The eagle's powerful feet are ideal for grabbing these very stout, rounded animals, which look like giant guinea pigs.

Black vulture foot

The New World vultures have feet more like a big chicken's than a bird of prey's. These feet have very little grip or power. The feet of Old World vultures are more powerful.

Soft feathering on owls' feet and legs helps keep them warm and silent

Vultures' talons do not need to be curved, because they are used for walking not for killing prey

Owl foot

Most owls have feathered toes to help with silent flying and landing. Owls, and ospreys, have a reversible outer toe. This toe sits forward when they relax, but is swung back when they grip something, to help them grasp their prey, or perches, better.

When owls' feet are relaxed, they have three toes pointing forward, and one pointing backward

African fish eagle foot

The osprey and all fish eagles have scaly feet. This helps them grasp a slippery fish—their main food source.

This foot is larger than a human hand

Talons more curved than other eagles'

Sparrowhawk leg

Sparrowhawks tend to catch small birds, such as sparrows, hence their name. They often snatch birds from the air. They have long, thin legs and toes, with needlelike talons, perfect for grasping their small, elusive prey.

The knee joint

The ankle joint

Long, thin bones give extra reach

Birds perch and walk on their toes, not their feet

Hunting techniques

Eagle eating a snake

Many open-country raptors hunt by flying high, surveying a wide area, then swooping fast. Eagles glide down quickly to take prey on the ground; falcons dive even faster to catch birds in midair. Harriers and owls hunt differently: they fly low and slow, looking and listening for quarry in the undergrowth. Many raptors, especially those in wooded areas, will "still hunt"—hunt from perches, sprinting out from cover when prey comes around the corner.

Still hunting

Buzzards and hawks, such as this red-tailed hawk (left), are very good at still hunting. They will sit and watch a rabbit until it strays too far from its hole. It is often the rabbit's last mistake.

Nictitating membrane often sweeps across to protect the bird's eye as it attacks

The perch must be inconspicuous; many raptors have a favorite perch that they use frequently

Some raptors flit from perch to perch as they hunt

Feet can lock onto prey so powerfully that sometimes raptors find it hard to release it

Dropping in for a bite

Some birds of prey, like this red-tailed hawk (above), will catch anything. The red-tailed hawk, or red-tailed buzzard as it is called in the UK, will hunt for small prey like this chipmunk, but it can also manage a full-grown rabbit. Other raptors, such as the snail kite, eat one particular prey.

Tail is spread out to act as a brake

Fishing eagles

Ospreys, fishing buzzards, fishing owls, and fish eagles, like this white-bellied fish eagle (left), live near the sea, lakes, and rivers and catch fish. With the exception of ospreys, which have a unique hunting technique, these birds usually sit on a high perch, watching the water for fish feeding on the surface.

Primary feathers fanned out to keep bird from stalling as it brakes rapidly

Hawks spot potential prey

One hawk swoops down to flush the prey out of cover

View to a kill

Eagle surveys wide areas

Most large eagles need wide, open spaces to fly in as they hunt. They often soar, looking for tiny movements, and then dive on their prey with deadly intent.

Eagle dives down on its quarry

Other hawks move into position to ambush prey

Stoop to conquer

All large falcons live in open country, and their prey can see them far away. To get extra speed, they climb high and stoop (dive) on their quarry, when it is far from cover.

Quarry driven into open

All in the family

Most raptors are solitary hunters. Sometimes breeding pairs hunt together. A few species work in teams. Harris' hawks hunt in family groups of up to six (right). Several birds may tackle the prey at once. If the prey is in cover, one or more birds may try to flush (frighten) it into the open. Together, the group can tackle larger prey than one bird could on its own.

The kill

Prey and feeding

Some raptors will eat anything, others are specialized feeders. The snail kite eats only snails, and the bearded vulture (left), eats mostly bones and marrow. Insects are very important to many birds of prey: 12 species eat only insects. A few species even eat fruit as well as meat, such as the palm nut vulture. The small, insect-eating birds must eat frequently, but many of the larger birds survive on one or two kills a day. Vultures may have to look for a long time for food, so they gorge themselves when they can: an 11 lb (5 kg) griffon vulture can eat nearly 4½ lb (2 kg) in one meal.

Bearded wonder
Bearded vultures are named for the beardlike feather tufts on their faces. They eat bones. They swallow small bones whole and drop large bones onto rocks from about 200 ft (60 m), sometimes more than 20 times, until they break.

Skin above beak becomes red when caracara is upset or excited

Empty crop

Pick of the crop
All the day-flying (diurnal) birds of prey have crops. Their food goes into the crop when they eat and is digested later. As they eat, the crop gradually bulges out.

Primary feathers are black, rest of bird is white

Black vultures draw their neck feathers down when they are feeding so they don't get blood over them

Vultures brace themselves on their legs to rip off meat

Bring a friend
It is thought that if black vultures (left) find a carcass whose skin is too tough for them to tear open, they will find a larger king vulture and lead it to the carcass. The king vulture rips it open and feeds, and the black vultures can then eat, too.

Skin above beak is usually yellow

Full crop; contrast empty crop of caracara on left

Caracaras will scavenge almost anything they find

Not welcome at the feast

Some raptors, such as this Cooper's hawk (right), "mantle" their food. That is, they spread their wings out above it as they eat, hiding it from other raptors.

Wings outspread to hide food look like a cloak, or mantle

Cooper's hawks eat small mammals and birds

Egg-shaped stones are preferred for throwing at ostrich eggs

Seasons of plenty

Each year, the bald eagles of North America's Pacific coast have a huge banquet as salmon come upriver, lay their eggs, and die. Other raptors benefit from occasional surges in the numbers of their prey. Snowy owls and rough-legged buzzards lay more eggs in years when their main prey, lemmings, have a population explosion.

Nostril, or nares, are not see-through in Egyptian and other Old World vultures, unlike New World vultures

Pacific salmon die after they have spawned (laid their eggs), so the bald eagles just have to drag their bodies out of the river

Bird-brain extraordinaire

Various raptors eat eggs if they find them, but Egyptian vultures are the only birds that use a tool to do so, and the only birds of prey known to use a tool at all. To break into an ostrich egg, they pick up small rocks and throw them at the egg until it breaks open. They pick up smaller eggs and throw them onto the ground. Other ingenious raptors include bearded vultures. In addition to dropping bones from a height to break them open and eat the marrow, they also drop tortoises to break open their shells.

Ostrich eggs are the largest eggs in the world

Heads and senses

Birds of prey have excellent eyesight to help them hunt food—at least two or three times better than ours. In one test, a buzzard saw small grasshoppers 330 ft (100 m) away. Some species may see even better—up to eight times better than humans. Raptors also hear very well, especially owls and some harriers.

Eye story
The eyes of a eurasian buzzard (skull above) can be as big as those of an adult human, although the human is 50 times heavier.

Protective eyebrow
Raptors, such as this ferruginous hawk, have a very obvious eyebrow called the "supraorbital ridge." This ridge may shade the eye from the sun when hunting, or protect it from injury.

Ears and speed
The ear hole, such as in this peregrine (left), is small, but important. Sound is used for calling, recognizing mates, and for locating prey.

Small brain tilts to fit into back of skull

Hole for the ear

The beautiful bite
Falcons, such as this saker falcon, have large heads for their size. All falcons have an extra serration on each side of the beak, called the "toral tooth." They use this, as well as their feet, for killing quarry.

Eyes and beak take up a lot of room; the brain is small

Toral tooth to kill prey

Eye wiper
The cloudy surface on the eye of this Verreaux's eagle (above) is a third eyelid called the "nictitating membrane." This membrane is a tough, clear skin that flicks across the eye to keep it clean, and is often closed on impact with prey to protect the eye.

The eagle can see as least twice as far as the man, probably farther

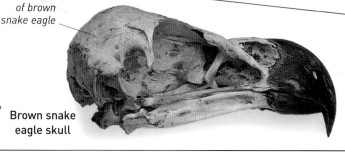

The uses of the tongue
Raptors, like this golden eagle (right), pant to lose heat. They breathe through a hole halfway along their tongues. They also use their tongues to hook back food from the tips of their beaks so they can swallow it.

Golden eagle loses heat through its tongue

Brain area of brown snake eagle

Great eyes, big brains
A golden eagle can see a rabbit at least 1 mile (1.6 km) away. The smartest birds of prey are the vultures, because they have the largest brains.

Brown snake eagle skull

Head turner
Birds of prey have such big eyes that they cannot move them in the sockets. Instead, they turn their heads with their long, flexible necks. They can even turn their heads to look at life from upside down.

Young African fish eagles have brown and white heads

This sub-adult bird's head is turning white, the color of an adult's head

Small brain

Eyes face forward, so that their fields of vision overlap (this is called binocular vision), which enables the bird to judge distance

Hunters' eyes face forward

Raptors have forward-facing eyes (see black kite skull above). This gives them the ability to judge depth and distance, which is essential if they are to hunt successfully.

Voice of Africa

African fish eagles use their loud calls to attract mates. Raptors use their voices in many ways, from chicks begging for food, to the excited calls made during aggressive encounters.

White-backed vultures are not really bald; the head and neck are covered in a fine down

Supraorbital ridge

Vulture's piercing eye scans wide areas for carcasses

No need for a knife and fork

Vultures, such as this white-backed vulture (above), have very strong necks and beaks to help them tear through the tough skin of large animals. Big vultures, such as the lappet-faced vulture in Africa and the Andean condor, can break through the skin on dead buffaloes and whales.

Crest is only half-extended

Thin but powerful beak

Turkey vultures can sniff out their food

Nares (nostrils) are completely see-through

Sending signals

Many birds of prey have a crest. It is thought a crest can signal a bird's mood. A raised crest probably means the bird is angry. Crests vary in length. The changeable hawk eagle (left) has a short crest.

A nose for food

The turkey vulture is the only bird of prey known to have a good sense of smell. It lives in the forests of the Americas and flies over the tree canopy trying to locate dead animals by smell.

Human sight is far weaker than that of an eagle

Skeletons

In some birds of prey, the skeleton weighs less than the total weight of the feathers. This lightness is necessary if the birds are to fly. Many of the larger bones are hollow and filled with air to make them light. At the same time, the skeleton has to be strong enough to anchor and support the bird's powerful flying muscles, and to protect its internal organs.

White-tailed
sea eagle

Wedge-tailed eagles have 14 cervical (neck) vertebrae

The coracoid links the sternum and the shoulder area

Shoulder muscles are attached to the scapula

Lower jaw can only move straight up and down; birds do not chew, they only bite and rip off chunks of flesh

The five thoracic vertebrae, in the center of the back above the synasacrum, are fused together

Bones of pelvis, lower back vertebrae, and most of tail vertebrae are fused in one unit of bone, called the synasacrum

Wedge-tailed eagle

Sternum

Knee joint

The caudal (tail) vertebrae give firm, yet flexible, support to the muscles of the tail; the last six vertebrae are fused

Tibia (lower leg bone) fused with some of the upper foot bones in the tibiotarsus

This is the bird's ankle

Anchors for muscles
The four bones of the pectoral girdle anchor the flight muscles: the shoulder muscles attach to the scapula, the breast muscles to the sternum and furcula (wishbone). The coracoid links shoulders and breast. This girdle is attached flexibly to the body, so that it can move easily as the bird flies.

Bones to fly with
Bird skeletons follow the same basic pattern as human skeletons, but some bones are fused together to give the rigidity needed to support the flight muscles. The bones of the pelvis are fused to give a strong platform for the leg and tail muscles.

White-tailed
sea eagle

Most foot bones are fused together in the tarsometatarsus, which acts as an extension of the leg

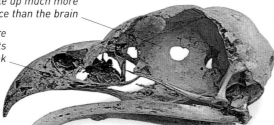

Eyes take up much more space than the brain

Jaws are lightweight struts to support beak

Secretary bird skull

Like a honeycomb
Although birds' major bones are hollow, they are strong. This is because they have internal struts across them (above). Such bones are called pneumatic bones, because they are filled with air, and some are attached to the air sacs of the bird's respiratory system.

Bones of skull are extensively fused to protect head with minimum of weight

Egyptian vulture skull

Look, ma, no teeth
Birds save weight by having no teeth and light jawbones. They can do this because "chewing" happens in the gizzard section of the stomach.

Sclerotic ring supports the huge eyeball

Golden eagle head

Better than a rubber neck
Humans have seven vertebrae in their necks; birds have from between 13 and 25, depending on the species. This long necks enable them to preen and clean virtually their whole bodies. It also gives them the ability to look around directly behind them.

Skull is paper-thin, yet very strong

This joint is the bird equivalent of the human wrist; the bones beyond it are the equivalent of the bones of the hand

Tendons from the main flight muscles attach to the humerus, which is short and strong enough to take the stress

Bird equivalent of human forearm

The two, paired clavicles form the furcula (wishbone)

Bird-hunting raptors have particularly long, slender toes

Sparrowhawk skeleton

The bones that would be hand bones in a human are fused together in the last section of the wing

Lighter than feathers
In smaller birds the skeleton is paper-thin in places, but can withstand high-speed flight and high-speed impact as the birds catch their prey.

Long, supple neck, which is supported by a complex muscle structure, enabling very precise movement

Vultures

Vultures are scavengers. They prevent disease by eating dead animals before they decay. In Africa, they eat more meat than all other predators put together. Vultures are good at soaring but bad at flapping flight, so most live in hot places or in mountainous areas, where there are plenty of thermals. There are two separate groups: New World vultures in the Americas, and Old World vultures elsewhere.

Neck tucked in to ruff of feathers

10-ft (3-m) wingspan

Condors
The Andean condor (above) soars above the Andes mountains of South America. Some can even glide right across to the Pacific coast, where they scavenge dead whales.

Home with a view
Many vultures breed in the mountains, such as at "Vulture Rock" in Spain (above). Some species nest alone in caves, others in large groups called "colonies."

New World vultures urinate over their legs and feet, perhaps to cool themselves

Juveniles have dark brown plumage, adults have white

Bright yellow face; neck not bare, unlike most vultures

Old World
Old World vultures are related to kites and eagles, whereas New World vultures are only distantly related to other birds of prey. The smallest of the Old World vultures are Egyptian vultures (above). There are two kinds: the Indian breed has yellow beaks, and the European and African breeds have black beaks.

New World
The turkey vulture is the smallest of the New World vultures. It is found from southern Canada to Argentina. It has a superb sense of smell, which it uses to sniff out dead animals in the forests of the Americas.

Wings outstretched to keep its balance

Turkey vulture gets its name from its red face

Neck feathers can be pulled down when the bird is hot or feeding, and pulled up when it is cold

New World vultures have chickenlike feet

The tail sticks up when it is doing its bouncing walk

The dropped head can mean different things, including aggression

Dinner party: no jacket required

Vultures gather in large numbers to eat large carcasses. In Africa, up to six different species may gather at once, plus rival scavengers, such as marabou storks. A large group of vultures can strip an antelope carcass bare in 30 minutes.

Marabou storks also eat carrion

Eurasian griffon skull

Upper mandible fixed to the skull

Lower mandible moves, much like our jaw

Watcher in the sky

All vultures have excellent daylight eyesight. As they soar, they watch for signs of death, and watch one another. If one bird starts to drop, its neighbors will then start to follow.

Huge wings give vultures their soaring ability

A white-backed vulture can eat over 2 lb (1 kg) of meat in two minutes

Common, but clean

White-backed vultures, the most common in Africa, have bare heads and necks because they put them inside carcasses. Feathered heads would get very mucky. All vultures love to keep clean.

Feet for walking

Some vultures like to walk. The American black vulture (below) bounces along on strong legs. When hunting for small dead animals, it spends much of its time on the ground.

Black vultures can run or bounce along at a fast pace

Vultures

Vultures have to be very tough to survive by eating dead food. Much of it has become so rotten in the heat that it would poison other animals. Vultures race to reach carcasses as soon as they can. They prefer fresh carrion, but they are well prepared to eat whatever they find. The juices in a vulture's stomach are much more acidic than in other animals. This acid kills the dangerous bacteria that may have infested the carrion. Some kinds of vulture also let their white, sloppy urine cover their legs. This not only helps to cool down their feet, but the acidic urine also sterilizes their skin after the vulture has been walking through putrid remains.

Not ready for takeoff

A vulture is a greedy bird, and its flexible crop, or throat pouch, bulges with food. After a big meal, the bird is often too heavy to fly away and simply goes to sleep until the food has been digested. However, if the vulture needs to get airborne, it will run with wings outstretched to catch the air, and in an emergency will throw up its meal to lighten the load.

Messenger to the gods

King vultures are the largest New World vultures, with a wingspan of almost 6½ ft (2 m). They live in the Amazon rain forest and the surrounding region. The adults have distinctive red, orange, and blue shading on their featherless heads and a red ring around the eye. In the stories of the ancient Maya people from Mexico, this vulture represented the god that carries messages between humans and the gods.

Powerful, hooked beak adapted for tearing open tough carcasses

Vulture hides

The behavior of vultures is predictable. They gather high in the sky above areas with powerful thermals and then fly down to wherever there is food. That makes it possible for bird-watchers to get a very good look at them. Vulture-watching stations, or hides, are located at the tops of cliffs to see flying birds. To watch them eat, bird-watchers go into hides sunk into the ground, and meat is placed outside to lure in the vultures.

One-way mirror allows the bird-watcher to see out, but the birds cannot see in

Huge wings spread wide to catch the thermal

Catching thermals

This griffon vulture (above) is on the lookout for its next meal, scanning the ground and sniffing the air for carcasses. To get a better view, it searches for thermals – warm currents of air that rise up the ground. The bird circles around inside a thermal, slowly rising higher and higher.

Fighting over scraps

Vultures are not the only animals that survive by eating carrion, and there is often a fight over food. A vulture will fight off a small scavenger, such as a jackal, but will normally back away if a larger animal, such as a lion, arrives. They wait until larger animals have finished eating and then pick at the scraps.

Jackal arches back and bears teeth to scare off vultures

Tower of silence

Vultures are important to Zoroastrians. Followers of this ancient religion from Central and southern Asia do not bury or cremate their dead. Instead, they place the dead bodies in a walled pit, called a Tower of Silence, and leave them to be eaten by vultures.

Ospreys and fish eagles

Ospreys are perfectly adapted for catching fish. To help them grip the fish, their talons are extra-curved, and they have scales on the soles of their feet as well as specially adapted toes. They soar high above the water to spot their prey, then dive steeply down to seize it. They are the only raptors that will go completely underwater to catch a fish. The eight species of fish eagle also catch fish, have extra-curved talons, and scaly soles to their feet, but they also scavenge, and will eat almost anything they catch. Unlike ospreys, fish eagles usually catch fish by still hunting.

Born to fish
Ospreys have long legs to help them catch fish under the water, and their outer toes can be swung backward to help them grip their slippery prey. Their plumage tends to be more waterproof than that of other raptors.

Osprey's wings sweep back in the final dive into the water

Arc of a diver
Ospreys usually take fish close to the water's surface. They can, however, plunge into the water. They soar, circle, and hover over water looking for quarry, then dive in, throwing their feet forward to snatch the fish.

Fish is held with its nose facing the front to reduce drag

Symbol of America
The bald eagle was chosen as the national emblem of the United States in 1782. Benjamin Franklin disapproved of the choice because bald eagles steal food from others. He believed the turkey should become the emblem. However, the eagle won the day.

Eagle holds olive branch to symbolize peace

Other foot holds arrows to symbolize war

Ospreys have narrow heads, with no bony ridges above their eyes

Sturdy nests withstand storms on exposed coasts

Family home
Ospreys use the same nest every year. It can become very big as it is added to each time. All sorts of materials are used, even bones. Some ospreys nest in reed beds or on the ground on treeless islands.

These eagles have loud and raucous voices

Varied diet
The white-bellied sea eagle lives along the coasts of India, southeast Asia, and Australia. It hunts fish, rabbits, bats, other birds, and even sea snakes.

Waiting for the feast

Every year, Pacific salmon swim upriver, lay their eggs, and then die. Bald eagles gather to feed on them in vast numbers. On one river in Alaska, it is possible to see up to 2,000 of them in the season.

The eagles just sit and wait for the salmon to die

Steller's sea eagle has an enormous beak

The eagle has landed, again

The white-tailed sea eagle (below) is one of the largest species of eagle. In Britain, it became extinct in 1916. However, in the 1960s, white-tailed sea eagles were released into the wild on a remote Scottish island. The bird is still rare in Britain, but its numbers are growing.

The big-beaked big brother

Steller's sea eagles are the largest of all the fish-eating birds of prey. They live on the coast of Russia and China and eat mainly Pacific salmon. They will also catch large birds, such as geese, and mammals, such as hares, and even young seals.

Supra-orbital ridge

This juvenile bird does not have the full adult plumage

Tail slowly turns white as eagle reaches adult breeding age

Powerful beak can tear through tough fish skin with ease

Sea eagle swallows bones with the flesh

Strong feet with rough scales to hold the slippery catch

Salmon are the favorite food of many northern eagles

Ospreys and fish eagles

The fish eagle group contains eight species, including the bald eagle from North America, Palla's fish eagle from Asia, and the African fish eagle. They belong to the genus *Haliaeetus*, which means sea eagle in Greek. While many of these species prey on freshwater fish, they are all found in coastal areas as well. The gray-headed fish eagle and the lesser fish eagle belong to a related genus *Ichthyophaga*, meaning fish-eater. These two Asian species only hunt in fresh water.

Not bald, nor bold, but "balde"

From a distance the bald eagle's white head looks as though it may be featherless, like a vulture's. However, a closer look shows that the head is covered in short and thick white feathers. Its name is derived from an old English word "balde," which means white-headed.

Rarest eagle

With a little more than 240 adults left in the wild, the Madagascan fish eagle is the rarest of the fish eagles. The species is critically endangered because local people living along the coasts kill and capture the birds, thinking they eat too many fish and make it harder for fishermen to make a living. The hope is that the last few fish eagle nests can be protected, and that people learn to look after these glorious hunters.

Head pale brown, not white like most fish eagles

Largest eagle in Madagascar with a wingspan of 6 ft (1.8 m)

Black wings in sharp contrast with white upper body and chestnut-colored belly

Ice eagle

Steller's sea eagle is one of the biggest raptors. It lives along the northern coast of the Asian Pacific, where the ocean can freeze over in winter. It is not unusual for animals that live in cold habitats to be larger than animals that live in warmer areas. A large body loses heat more slowly than a smaller one. However, Steller's sea eagle cannot hunt easily in freezing water, so it migrates south in winter.

Distinctive white patches or "shoulders"

Tank eagle

The gray-headed fish eagle lives in India, Sri Lanka, and across Southeast Asia. It does not fly much and spends most of its time perching over slow-moving waters, watching for prey. It eats mostly fish, but will also grab any snakes and mammals it spots in the water. This eagle is especially common around reservoirs or other artificial "tanks" of water, and so it is also known as the tank eagle.

Satellite tracker fitted on the back

Tracking ospreys

Some ospreys are fitted with satellite-tracked backpacks before they migrate to spend the winter in Africa or South America. Scientists use trackers to figure out what route the birds take and where they stop to rest along the way. Protecting these resting areas is crucial, because the birds use them to find their way. Without them, the ospreys get lost and cannot meet up to breed at the right times.

African fish eagle

This big hunter can be seen catching fish in rivers and lakes all over Africa, south of the Sahara Desert. It sometimes catches a fish that is too heavy to haul back into the air, so it drags it across the surface to the nearest shore. With even larger prey, the eagle lands on the water and paddles to the shore with its wings, holding the fish firmly with its talons.

Dark, hooked beak

Highly curved talons help to grip slippery prey

Kites and harriers

Kites are easily recognized by their forked tails. There are 33 species. The largest is the European red kite; the smallest, the South American pearl kite. Many of the smaller species eat insects, others hunt for larger quarry, some are scavengers, and some even fish. The 13 species of harrier, and three related species, have huge wingspans and light bodies, which allow them to fly very slowly while looking for prey.

Swallow-tailed kite in flight

Male drops food to female

Aerobatic lunch
After hunting, the male harrier calls to the female, who flies to meet him. He drops the food, which she catches, and takes back to the nest. The male then hunts again.

African harrier hawk has a large crest and bare face

Color of back feathers is different in juveniles

Harriers often nest in reeds, tussocky grass, or even standing crops

No high-rise here
Most harriers, like the hen harrier (above), build nests on the ground. Harriers usually lay three to four eggs, but can have up to 10. Kites usually build messy nests in trees.

Adaptable bird
Black kites are found in many areas of the world. Their diet includes mice, rats, fish, frogs, and carrion. Like many kites, they fly in large flocks where food is abundant, but nest alone.

Long thin legs and toes are ideal for pushing into cracks and holes to find food

Cradle snatcher

Three species of raptor are closely related to harriers. The African harrier hawk looks very similar, with huge wings and a small body weight. Its ankle is double-jointed (bends both backward and forward), which helps it to get its foot into holes in cliffs and hollow trees, to hook out baby birds to eat. It flies very slowly through trees, looking for likely holes to raid. A similar bird, the crane hawk, found in South American forests, hunts the same way.

Part of the family

Yellow-billed kites are the African subspecies of the black kite. They are a slightly different color and have a yellow bill (beak).

Kites can twist and turn in an amazing fashion

Most kites have a forked tail; in some species it is much more forked than this

Red kite has a pale iris

Slowly does it

Harriers hunt by flying low and slow over marsh, moor, and grasslands. They listen for sounds in the grass and eat prey up to the size of a small rabbit.

Harriers sometimes fly at a height of less than 3 ft (1 m) as they hunt

Success story

A number of raptors suffered huge declines in recent decades, largely due to pesticides. A number of species have recovered, however. The red kite was once common in Britain, then was reduced to a small, population in Wales. It has been reintroduced in England and Scotland, and is now thriving.

Large flocks of kites will scavenge for food on garbage dumps

Reddish color of feathers gives the red kite its name

Long tail aids slow flying

Not fussy, nor fearful

Kites are not afraid of humans—in Africa, some even snatch sandwiches from people's hands when they eat outside. Kites will go into garbage dumps to find scraps to eat. However, they run the risk of picking up poisonous food or getting pieces of plastic caught around them.

Kites are easy to identify in flight by their forked tails

Kites and harriers

Both kites and harriers are known for their large wingspan compared to their body sizes. These allow both birds to fly more slowly than other raptors. However, harriers and kites fly in different ways. Harriers are low-flying birds that make swoops over grasslands and shrubs in search of prey. Kites, which are bigger than harriers, tend to fly much higher and soar in wide circles as they scan the ground for prey or carrion. Many kites can also hover in the air above their targets.

Letter wings

The letter-winged kite from Australia is named after the dark stripe under its wings. When the kite is soaring overhead, the kinked stripes on both wings make the letter "M." However, it is rare to see this mostly nocturnal bird.

Dark, black stripes make an "M" when wings are outstretched

Scorched feathers

The swamp harrier is the largest and most common bird of prey in New Zealand. When the Māori people arrived in New Zealand several centuries ago, they cleared areas of forests to make way for their villages. This created a good hunting habitat for the swamp harrier. The Māoris call the bird Kāhu and see it as a good omen.

Males are gray-black, while females are dark brown

Apple snails make up most of the snail kite's diet

Snail hunter

The snail kite of South America feeds almost entirely on water snails scooped up from rivers and swamps. The bird flies slowly over water as it searches for food. It swoops in and grabs the snail with its claws, carrying it back to a perch. The kite then uses its slender, hooked beak to pull the soft snail from its shell.

Pirates aloft

This short-eared owl is about to lose its lunch to the marsh harrier. While marsh harriers are able hunters, they are also known to steal food from other birds. This kind of behavior is called "pirating," and marsh harriers use their flying skills to snatch food from the feet of other birds of prey. However, harriers need to watch out—larger raptors, such as eagles, will also try to steal food from them.

Harrier flies underneath the owl and grabs the vole

Gray glider

The plumbeous kite of the Amazon rain forest gets its name from the Latin word *plumbum*, meaning lead. When perching, the bird appears gray, or lead-colored, all over, with its bright-red legs and feet poking out from its feathers. When it is in flight, however, a reddish patch is revealed on the underside of the wings, near the tips.

Whistling killer

The whistling kite of Australasia gets its name from the loud calls it makes. It normally produces a long whistle that rises in pitch and then a series of loud single notes. The kite calls from perches and nests, but also while flying. Flying calls are used during courtship, and to warn off rivals. As it calls, the kite swoops with curved wings and spreads its flight feathers.

Hawks and buzzards

North American Swainson's hawks, like other hawks, often hunt from man-made perches

Hawks live mostly in forests. They are fast-flying and agile, with short, rounded wings that help them twist and turn quickly through trees as they chase quarry. Buzzards are very adaptable. They live in a wide range of habitats, especially part-wooded and cultivated land.

Long legs

There are about 20 species of buzzard around the world, including the long-legged buzzard (left). They all have thick legs and strong feet—ideal for catching small mammals.

Best of hunters

In medieval Europe, the goshawk was known as the "cook's bird," since it caught so much food with which to fill the pantry. Because they are slower than hawks and easier to train, buzzards were probably used to train apprentice falconers.

Harris' hawks tend to fly more slowly (and use their brains more) than true hawks

Sparrowhawk plucks feathers from blackbird before eating it

Don't eat the feathers

Hawks pluck the feathers from their prey before eating. They often have "plucking posts" near their nests, where they take prey to pluck it. Hawks are divided into the (larger) goshawks and the (smaller) sparrowhawks. Goshawks hunt both "fur and feather"—both mammals and birds; sparrowhawks usually catch small birds.

Hawklike tail and wings give great agility

Hawks can take relatively big prey: female sparrowhawks catch wood pigeons that are heavier than they are, as well as blackbirds such as this

Hawks often use hedges and trees as cover as they fly toward prey, only "breaking cover" and showing themselves at the last moment

Feeding the kids

In Britain, the number of European buzzards (above) crashed when most rabbits died from myxomatosis, then rose as rabbit numbers recovered.

Hawk or buzzard?

The Harris' hawk falls between the hawk and buzzard families. It has the characteristic hawk shape, but resembles buzzards in its relaxed temperament. It is unusually sociable. It hunts in groups and breeds cooperatively: parents are helped in rearing chicks by other Harrises in the group.

Alula, or "false wing," helps with stopping and low-speed flight

Harris' hawks are also called bay-winged hawks because of the brown color on the tops of their wings

The larger hawks have strong legs; the smaller sparrowhawks, which prey on birds not mammals, have thinner, less strong legs with very long toes

Hawks and buzzards

The English word hawk comes from the old German word for "to grab" or "to seize." It relates to the exceptional hunting ability of these birds, grabbing prey as they twist and turn through woodlands. Buzzard comes from a French word for hawk, and the "-ard" has been added to indicate that these birds are inferior, or less-able, than other "true" hawks. Buzzards lack the high-speed hunting skills of hawks and will make do with a wider range of food, including carrion.

Most of the water falls out of the mouth before the bird can swallow it

Sipping a drink

A hawk's hooked beak is built for delivering a killer bite, but its shape makes it difficult for the bird to drink water. The hawk cannot lap up water either, because the opening of the windpipe is in the tongue. The bird will take little sips of water occasionally and then throw its head back so some water can trickle down its throat.

Stone is used to crack open thick emu egg shells

The brown feathers of this young bird will turn black as it grows old

Egg smasher

The Australian black-breasted buzzard (left) hunts small animals and also steals eggs. It cracks small eggs with its beak, but bigger ones, like those of the emu, have harder shells. The bird dive-bombs the nest and drops a large stone from its mouth, repeating the attack until the egg cracks.

Stashing food

During the breeding season, goshawks create a food store up a tree. They wedge prey in a high fork, out of the reach of climbing predators, such as black bears and martens. The birds generally leave the food for only a few hours, returning later to feed it to their young. A goshawk pair will fiercely defend both the nest and food supply from any animal that comes close.

Rabbit will be stashed in the tree for only a few hours

Scaly feathers protect the bird from stings

Horus is always seen wearing a pharaoh's crown

Twilight hunter

As the sun sets, bats begin to emerge from their roosts for a night of hunting. The bat hawk (above) is ready for them. This small raptor chases bats in a high-speed pursuit. Its long wings allow the bird to accelerate up behind its prey, and it grabs the bat in its slender, sharp talons. While still flying, the prey is then transferred to the small beak, where it is killed with a bite.

Guardian of the pharoah

The ancient Egyptian god Horus is most often shown as a man with the head of a hawk or falcon. Horus was the sky god, and his name means the "one above" or the "distant one." Horus was also sometimes seen as a war god, and his eye was said to watch over the pharaoh and keep him safe.

Nest raider

This honey buzzard (above) has stolen a piece of honeycomb from a bees' nest. Despite its name, the raptor will not eat the honey. Instead, it scoops out the grublike bee larvae growing in the honeycomb's hexagonal cells. The bird has especially long toes to dig down into underground nests. It can also attack wasps and hornets.

Eagles

The eagle is seen as the king of the birds. There are over 40 species of eagle, and several distinct groups. The forest eagles include the South American harpy eagles, which are probably the most powerful of all raptors. The true eagles live in open country. Some, such as golden eagles, can have wingspans of over 8 ft (2.5 m). Forest eagles have shorter, more rounded wings and longer tails than true eagles.

Child snatcher?

Many eagles have been seen feeding on prey much bigger than anything they could kill. However, despite the the stories of eagles carrying off children, there is no verified record of an eagle killing a child.

Jungle eagle

Most forest eagles, such as the African hawk eagle (right), belong to the family of hawk eagles. These birds are a similar shape to hawks. They can turn very fast, and so can hunt successfully amid thick trees.

Striped breast feathers act as camouflage when eagle sits in trees

Common pirate

Tawny eagles mainly scavenge. They often act as "pirates," chasing other raptors that have just caught prey and stealing it.

All true eagles have feathers down to their toes, as do some forest eagles

Feathers down to their toes give the name "booted eagles"

Eagle spreads wings to make it look larger and more threatening

Warthog is defending its baby from the eagle

Imperial symbol

Eagles have been the symbols of many great empires, including ancient Rome, the Russia of the czars, and the Austrian Habsburg empire. Roman legions used to carry eagle standards as their symbols and rallying-points (above). To lose the legion's eagle was the worst of all possible disasters.

Birds often pick a dead branch high up as a look-out point

Baby warthog snatcher

Giant martial eagles are the biggest of all the African eagles. They have huge feet and are powerful enough to kill jackals and small antelopes, let alone baby warthogs. They live in open country, on the plains of Africa, and swoop down from the air to catch their prey.

Nictitating membrane protects and cleans eye

Family home
Golden eagles return to the same nest sites year after year to raise their young (right). Good nesting sites stay in use: when one pair stops breeding, another will take over the nest.

Chicks cheep to stimulate their mother to feed them

Brown plumage of young bateleur changes gradually into adult plumage

Gold-colored feathers on back of head and neck give golden eagle its name

Acrobat of the air
A dull brown juvenile bateleur eagle (above) grows into a brightly colored adult (left). They were given the name "bateleur," which means balancer, because they are so acrobatic in the air.

Religious raptor
The eagle is a religious symbol in many cultures, from Native American to Indian. In Christianity, the eagle came to be a symbol of John the evangelist (above), one of Jesus' first disciples.

Fork halfway along tongue helps bird pull food into throat

Some golden eagles have wingspans of more than 8 ft (2.5 m)

Contour feathers give shape to wing

Stocky build is characteristic of golden eagles

Golden eagles help farmers by killing rabbits, which compete with sheep for grass

This 4½ lb (2 kg) rabbit will last the 9 lb (4 kg) eagle for two days

Moderate eater
Golden eagles live in the tundra areas of the northern hemisphere. Like most eagles, they kill small prey, such as rabbits, although they may scavenge on large dead animals.

Continued from previous page

Eagles

Eagles live all over the world, but the great majority are based in Africa and Eurasia. There are 60 eagle species in these regions, but only 14 living in the Americas and Australasia. However, wherever they are, eagles are always the top flying predator. Many birds of prey are at risk of being preyed upon themselves, and are always on the lookout for threats. Because adult eagles have no natural predators, they do not display this behavior. They keep their young safe in vast nests called aeries, which are either built at the tops of trees or on cliff ledges, far out of reach from attack by climbing predators.

Crested serpent eagle

As its name suggests, this eagle preys mostly on snakes, but it will also prey on whatever else it spots in shallow water, including crabs and eels. It lives in the wetland areas of India and Southeast Asia, where snakes are common. It is a still hunter, meaning it perches, often out of sight, on a branch, waiting still for many hours until it sees prey moving below.

Snake is killed with a bite and then taken back to a perch

Haast's eagle

The largest bird of prey ever known to exist, called Haast's eagle, lived in New Zealand until the 13th century. It weighed 30 lb (14 kg) and had a wingspan of 8½ ft (2.6 m). It is thought Haast's eagle was an ambush hunter that swooped on prey from a hiding place in the trees above. The eagle became extinct because its main prey, the giant moa, was wiped out by the Māori people, who had recently arrived on the islands.

Performing eagle

The bateleur (right) is an African eagle. Its name means "street performer" in French. This bird is quite the showman, with bright red legs and beak. It makes spectacular aerial performances during courtship and slaps its wings together to make a loud snapping noise. During attack runs, the bird flies fast and low, rocking its wings as if balancing on a tightrope. It also likes to sunbathe and holds its wings out to catch the sun's heat.

Vishnu's mount

The Javan hawk-eagle is one of the national symbols of Indonesia, where it is known as the garuda. Garuda is a half-man and half-bird creature from Hindu mythology, ridden by Lord Vishnu. Garuda is the archenemy of Naga, a mythical water snake, much like the real-life Javan eagle, which often preys on snakes in its rain forest habitat.

A plasterwork decoration of Indonesia's national symbol

Personal eagles

Bonelli's eagle (left) lives in wooded highland habitats, from southern Europe to Indonesia. It is named after Franco Andrea Bonelli, an Italian ornithologist, who discovered the bird in 1822. There are many other eagles named after their discoverers, or to honor famous naturalists. Verreaux's eagle, from southern Africa, is named for Frenchman Jules Verreaux, who brought the first specimen to Europe in the 18th century.

Short, rounded wings help the bird steer a course through the branches

Monkey eater

The harpy eagle of Central America and the Amazon rain forest is the largest eagle in the Americas, and one of the largest raptors in the world. This heavy hunter does not fly long distances, but makes swooping attacks high in the trees. It almost never comes to the ground. Instead, the eagle snatches monkeys and other mammals, such as sloths, that live in the branches.

The secretary bird

Two-week-old secretary bird

The same bird at six weeks old

Secretary birds have long legs, a hooked beak, and, like all birds of prey, they kill with their feet. They live in grasslands, desert edges, or farmed land in Africa, south of the Sahara. They need a flat-topped tree to nest in, but they cannot live in forests because it is too tricky for them to take off and fly amid the trees. They also avoid very thick, tall grass. They flush out prey by walking through the long grass, and then kill it by stamping on it. Famous for killing snakes, they also eat a wide variety of insects, small animals, and birds.

What's in a name?

Some think the name comes from the Arabic *saqr-tair*,—"hunting bird." Others believe the feathers on the birds' heads looked like secretaries with quills behind their ears (above).

The young secretary bird

When first hatched, young secretary birds have huge heads. Their legs grow so fast that the scales can't keep up, and in the first few days the old scales split off and new scales grow again and again. They cannot stand up until almost full-grown, which means that they cannot fall out of the nest until they are ready to fly, or at least glide. Secretary birds are thriving in the wild. They are valuable to farmers because they kill snakes and rodents, although some people still hunt them.

Primary feathers are black; secretary birds can fly and soar very well when they want to

Long quill-like crest feathers

Eyelashes are longer and more beautiful than any human's

Facial skin goes bright orange as bird matures

Slides down nicely

Secretary birds swallow snakes whole, slowly sucking them in. They have a unique method of killing prey, but, as with all raptors, it involves their feet. They stamp on their quarry, repeatedly if necessary. When killing insects they hit with any part of the foot, but when tackling snakes they strike with the back talon at the head of the snake, which is its most vulnerable, yet also most dangerous, part.

The two center tail feathers are twice as long as the rest

Scales protect the long, powerful legs from snakebites

Back toe used when striking snakes' heads

Crest raised, quill feathers up

Crest not raised, quill feathers down

Domestic bliss

Secretary birds will not even attempt to breed unless the food supply is plentiful. They lay two to three eggs, but usually only one chick survives. In some pairs, both parents take turns to incubate the eggs.

High-rise homes

Secretary birds build their nests on top of flat-topped trees. First, the birds trample the top until it is completely squashed, and then they add sticks and twigs to make a platform, which can be up to 8 ft (2.5 m) across. Tufts of grass and reeds are used to make a soft lining. Some nests are used year after year.

Locust

Lizard

Egg

Mouse

Chick

Buffet lunch

Snakes form only a small part of a secretary's diet. The bulk of their food consists of insects, such as grasshoppers, locusts, and large beetles. They also catch lizards, hedgehogs, mongooses, birds, rats, mice, and other mammals up to the size of a small hare. Eggs and baby birds are also on the menu. All but the largest items are swallowed whole.

Till death do us part

Once secretary birds have found a mate, they usually stay together for life. Unlike most raptors, they stay living in their nest together all year, not just when breeding. The paired birds tend to stay within sight of each other during the day, hunting, walking, and flying together, unless the female is brooding eggs or young.

Grass snake disappearing down secretary bird's throat; a good supper

The falcon family

The hobby can catch swifts in midair

The big falcons—sakers, lanners, peregrines, and gyrfalcons—are probably the fastest-flying of all the birds of prey and, when they stoop (dive), the fastest birds in the world. They live in open country, such as desert edges, tundra, moor, and grasslands. There are also various smaller true falcons, including kestrels, forest falcons, pygmy falcons, and falconets.

Game bird being struck in midair

Falcon stoops past after strike

Catching prey
Many falcons catch their prey by stooping down at high speed behind it, and then striking it in midair. Sometimes a falcon will grasp the prey in the air, called "binding to it." However, often the falcon will pick up the dead bird on the ground or catch it in midair before it hits the ground.

Caracaras have a different wing-shape from that of falcons

The odd relatives
Caracaras are closely related to falons. They scavenge and will often annoy campers in the Andes by stealing their food.

Bars of youth
A falcon's juvenile plumage has downward bars on the chest, and the shoulders and back feathers have buff edging. Falcons born in hot countries often look much paler than those hatching in cooler ones, because the sun bleaches out the color in the feathers.

Breast of immature lanner

Juvenile male lanner

Notch, or tooth, on falcon's beak

Adult male lanner

Spots of adult plumage

Flying hunter
Lanners live in some parts of Europe and the Middle East, and all over Africa, except for the rain forest and the Sahara. They catch small birds, insects, small mammals, and reptiles. They are numerous in Africa, but rare in Europe. A program in Israel to breed them and release them into the wild is doing well.

Short tail means falcons can't maneuver as well as hawks

Side view of juvenile to show back feathers

Side view of adult to show back feathers

Peregrine falcon nesting on a cliff ledge

Kestrels are a common sight in many towns

Choosing a home

Falcons don't build nests. Smaller falcons use disused nests or holes in trees. Larger falcons tend to use ledges on cliffs, rocks, or buildings.

Young members of the Mauritius kestrel

Taking time to look around

The 13 species of kestrel around the world are all able to hover. This enables them to "perch" in midair, giving them time to spot small animals on the ground. As a result, they are able to catch more small mammals than the other falcons.

Bird about town

Kestrels, and some other falcons, have learned that high-rise buildings are like cliffs, with ledges and alcoves that make good nesting places. They have also learned that where humans live there is often a plentiful supply of food.

Nowhere to run to

Mauritius kestrels almost became extinct because of the destruction of the forests on their home island. A breeding and release program has saved them, for now.

Unisex feathers?

In some raptors, males and females have different color plumage. Usually the difference doesn't show until the birds have their adult plumage. American kestrels are one exception: the difference is obvious as soon as they have feathers.

This dark bar is called the mustachial strip

Adult female lanner

Crop area is often less marked than the lower breast

Contour feathers have buff edges in immature plumage

Sub-adult female lanner

Juvenile stripes are lost in the first molt, after which the bird is sub-adult

Falcons' toes are even longer than hawks' toes

Individual markings

There is a certain amount of variation in plumage within each species. Individuals differ and so, in many species, do birds from different regions. Adult lanners from southern Africa have a pink breast with no markings; northern lanners tend to be very heavily marked.

Tail feathers are used in steering, and as brakes

The falcon family

It is thought the falcons form a separate group from other birds of prey. They are more closely related to parrots and songbirds than to other raptors. The oldest falcon fossils are only 10 million years old, but other raptor fossils go as far back as 47 million years. Falcons always kill with their beaks, while most other raptors use their feet. Their nestling habits are also different. Falcons lay eggs on simple scrapes. Another major anatomical difference is the tubercle in a falcon's nostril. This spike of bone stops air from rushing into the windpipe during high-speed dives.

Last raptor

The New Zealand falcon, also known as the kārearea, is the only endemic raptor left in New Zealand. It is much smaller than the more common swamp harrier, which also lives in New Zealand (and elsewhere).

Wing tips are pointed, which is typical of a falcon

White breast feathers, flecked with gray

Ready for the cold

The gyrfalcon (left) spends the summer around the edges of the Arctic. Even in summer it can be cold here, and the falcon has feathers covering its legs. While it perches, the bird pulls one of its feet into the thick feathers on its belly to save heat. Most gyrfalcons look silvery, but the groups in the north are paler to help hide among the snow, while those in the south are browner.

Foot tucked in feathers to keep warm

Insect eaters

The falconet (left) is not only the smallest falcon but also the smallest raptor. Falconets live in Asia and do not grow much bigger than a sparrow. These little hunters prey on flying insects, such as butterflies and dragonflies, using rapid wing beats followed by short glides as they fly through the forest.

The upper spike and lower notch is known as the tomial tooth

Laughing falcon

The laughing falcon (right) from South America gets its name from its *haw-haw-haw* call, which can sound eerily like a person laughing. Sometimes the call can suddenly drop in pitch, which makes the bird sound rather sad. A specialist snake hunter, it swoops down and pounces on poisonous snakes and kills them with a swift bite to the back of the head.

Killer tooth

Most falcons, such as the lanner falcon (above) from Africa and western Asia, have a second hooked feature on their beaks, which helps them deliver a killer bite. Behind the fearsome hook, the upper beak has a triangular spike. This slots into a notch on the lower beak.

Yellow ring surrounds the eye

Flight feathers spread out during slow, soaring flight

Father of a nation

A falcon plays an important role in the history of the Magyars, or Hungarian, people. The bird, known as Turul, is said to have fathered the first leader of the Magyars and declared that the tribe would move west from their original home in central Russia.

Rounded tail helps while soaring

Statues of Turul, such as this one, are common in Hungary

Owls

Most owls, though not all, hunt at night or at dawn and dusk. They hunt by stealth, flying slowly, softly, and silently to surprise their prey. They rely on their ears more than their eyes to find their quarry. They range in size from the tiny elf owl, which weighs only 1½ oz (40 g), up to the European eagle owl, which is a huge 6½ lb (3 kg). They fill almost all the hunting roles of day-hunting raptors, except for the fast flying and diving of the falcons, and scavenging.

Baby owls are soon able to swallow their food, such as this mouse, whole

Midnight caller
The tawny owl has the most famous of owl calls—"too-witt-too-woo." It also makes a shrill "kee-wick" noise late at night. It still hunts: it sits motionless, listening and looking out for movement, and then it pounces.

Silent eagle of the night
Owls fly on large, silent wings. Their feathers have a fine down all over them, and the leading edges of the outer flight feathers are serrated like a comb. This gives a soft, frayed edge that deadens the noise of their wingbeats, so their prey does not hear them coming.

All feathers are covered in a fine down

Bengal eagle owl

Mottled breast feathers aid camouflage and keep the bird warm in cold weather

Eagle owls have feathered toes, which help protect their feet from bites

Hooting boobook
The boobook owl gets its name from the hooting noise it makes. Several other kinds of owl are named after the sounds they make. The saw-whet owl, for example, makes a noise like a saw being sharpened.

Boobook owl's coloring helps to camouflage it during the daytime

Baby owls are covered in a fluffy down to keep them warm

Barn owls help farmers by killing mice and rats

Farmer's friend

Because they have a more pronounced disk-shaped face than other owls, barn owls have better sight and hearing. There are about 12 species found around the world. They often live on farms, because there are lots of mice and rats to hunt. They are known for living in barns, but anywhere secure, weatherproof, and quiet will do.

Baby owls

Baby owls in the same brood can be very different sizes. The mother bird starts sitting on the eggs almost as soon as she has laid the first one, so there can be a large gap between the oldest baby and the youngest.

White feathers camouflage owl in snow

Daytime owl

Some owls have to hunt in the day when raising chicks. In the Arctic, where the snowy owl (above) lives, the days are so long in the summer there is no night.

Owl's huge eye is easily damaged

Secondary feathers

Primary feathers

On the defensive

Owls, such as this long-eared owl (left), can be very fierce when defending themselves or their nests. To look fierce, they spread their wings and turn them around so the back faces the front (left). This makes them look much bigger than they really are.

For many owls, a vole such as this is a favorite food

Down in one

Owls like to swallow their prey whole, especially if it is small enough. Most owls eat rodents. Many owls live on insects. Spectacled owls eat crabs, eagle owls catch rabbits, hares, and even day-flying raptors as they rest at night.

Sitting pretty

Owls, such as this scops owl (above), perch differently from other birds of prey.

The life of owls

Owls do not build their own nests. Some use holes in trees, others use abandoned buildings, or barns, or even bridges, or take over abandoned nests. One species, the ferocious great horned owl, sometimes even takes over inhabited hawks' nests, killing the occupants. Owls tend to hide and rest during the day.

Wise as an owl

For centuries, owls have been thought of as being very wise. The owl was associated with Athena, the Greek goddess of wisdom.

Owl pellets

Contents of pellets

The eyes of a hunter

Owls have huge eyes at the front of their heads, as do other hunters, such as lions. Because their eyes are close together, hunting animals have binocular vision. This means they can judge depth and distance very well—vital when hunting. Their field of vision, however, is limited.

Eagle owl skull

Scleral ring, a bony ring that protects most of the eye

Bringing up dinner

Like many other birds, owls cough up pellets after they have eaten. They swallow indigestible parts of their quarry, such as fur, bones, and feathers. Their stomachs make these parts into a bundle that the owl coughs up.

The burrowing owl can make a noise like a rattlesnake to scare predators away from their holes

Going underground

Most owls are solitary, but burrowing owls live in colonies. They nest in old ground squirrel and prairie dog mounds in North America. Burrowing owls have a smaller facial disk than most owls, because they are mainly diurnal (active in the day), so have less need for extra-fine hearing and sight than nocturnal owls.

Burrowing owl looks out for danger on top of mound

Burrow can be only 4 in (10 cm) wide

Burrowing owl has longer legs for its body size than any other owl

Owls' senses

Owls are famous for their ability to see in the dark. They cannot see in total darkness, but need only the tiniest bit of light. Their hearing is even better. Owls have long ear openings, which can be almost as long as the owl's head. In some owls, one of the ears is much higher on the bird's head than the other. This makes it easier for the owl to work out where a sound is coming from.

Another way to look at life

Owls can turn their heads in every direction

An owl can turn its head over 360°

If they start facing forward, owls can turn their heads 270° each way

Ear tufts are nothing to do with ears; they are probably used to signal moods, such as anger or fear

Facial disk gathers light and sound into eyes and ears

What a dish
The shape of their faces helps owls, such as this Bengal eagle owl (right), to see and hear so well. They have a facial disk, or dish, that funnels all available light and sound into their eyes and ears.

Tawny owl with head turned

Mouth larger than size of beak suggests

Continued from previous page

Owls

Although they are birds of prey, owls are entirely unrelated to raptors. However, the evolution of the owl group, the Strigiformes, is something of a mystery. It is generally thought that owls evolved from the same ancestors as similar nocturnal birds, such as nightjars and pottos, but no one is certain. The owl fossil record goes back 58 million years, and most fossil specimens resemble modern barn owls. The other owls appear much later, around 23 million years ago. Fossils show that some ancient barn owls living on islands were more than 3 ft (1 m) tall and had become flightless ground hunters.

Most species have prominent "ear" tufts

White and black feathers create a silver-gray, camouflaged plumage

Bark camouflage

The screech owl (left) spends the day snoozing in holes and hollows in the trunks of trees. It is a master of disguise, with plumage matching the flaky bark of its daytime hideaway. When its big yellow eyes are closed, the bird blends in very effectively. Screech owls live across North and South America and their color varies between grays and reddish hues, depending on the type of tree trunks in which they live.

Right ear points up

Nostrils normally hidden by fluffy feathers

Left ear points down

Asymmetrical ears

Like most other vertebrates, an owl's ears are on either side of the head. However, unlike other animals, the right ear is higher up on the owl's skull than the left. Having two ears allows an animal to pick up the direction of sounds. A sound from the left reaches the left ear before the right one, and the brain can use the time difference to work out the direction.

Fake face

Owl butterflies play an amazing trick on predators. When they perch, the butterflies fold their wings above the body, so only the undersides are visible. If a predator comes close, the butterfly snaps open its wings to reveal the upper surface, which is adorned by two large eyespots. The sudden appearance of what looks like an owl can care off the predator.

Eyespot has a dark center, surrounded by pale ring

Small hooked beak is used to snatch insects from the air

Elf owl

This little hunter (left) is the world's smallest owl, weighing just 1½ oz (40 g) and measuring barely 5½ in (14 cm) long. It lives in the dry scrublands of Mexico and the Southwestern United States, where it raids the flowers of cacti for sleeping insects and scorpions. It seems to be unaffected by the stings of scorpions.

Head moves to mimic living owl

Owl decoys

Owls are well-known nighttime hunters. Even other bird species avoid places where they spot an owl on a perch. Large buildings, such as parking garages and airport terminals, often have problems with flocks of birds roosting inside, so model owls—some of which even have moving heads—are installed to scare the unwanted birds away.

More pork

The morepork owl lives in the forests of New Zealand and Tasmania. It is sometimes called the ruhu, but its more common name refers to its strange cries of "More pork! More pork!" The Māori people of New Zealand think the owl is the spirit of a wise spirit that lives in the forest.

Raptors in history

Raptors are important symbols in ancient cultures all over the world, and in many religions. The eagle represents authority, strength, victory, and pride and is linked with the sun, royalty, and gods. The owl may symbolize wisdom, or, because it is a bird of the night, may be linked with death and ill fortune, its cry an evil omen. More practically, people have hunted with raptors since ancient times.

Indian falconer
This 17th-century falconer was part of an ancient tradition. Falconry is known to have been practiced from the 2nd century CE in the Indian subcontinent, but it may have been practiced much earlier.

Coffin for falcon mummy; the designs are just like those on human mummy cases

Mummified falcon
Many ancient Egyptian gods and goddesses were linked with animals and birds. Some were even kept in temples to represent these deities. Falcons, such as the one above, were mummified and buried in tombs with kings.

Falconers' gloves have traditionally been made of strong leather to stop talons puncturing the hand beneath

Eagle feathers

Training horses to stand having raptors this close is not easy

William brought several species of raptor with him that had not been seen in England before

Early birds
This picture comes from the Bayeux tapestry, woven to celebrate William the Conqueror's conquest of England in 1066. The first English falconer was probably an 8th-century Saxon king of Kent, Ethelbert II.

Painted plaster mask for a falcon mummy

The Cooper's hawk is almost vertical as it comes in to land

This was worn on a lip plug, which was inserted through a hole made in the bottom lip

Facial charm
Jewelry and statues have often been made in the image of birds of prey. Eagle heads, like the one (above), were made as lip ornaments by the Mixtecs of Mexico, who made most of the gold work for the famous Aztec empire.

The actual falcon mummy

Hunting straps, a modern invention

Hawk magic
Falconry has appealed to people in many different cultures throughout history. Today, although falconry is no longer needed to provide food, it is still practiced as a sport.

The Cooper's hawk throws its legs up high to cushion the impact of landing

Eagles and the spirit
Eagles have long been objects of worship to North American Indians. Their feathers were used in many decorative ways, most famously on headdresses. This eagle feather wand (left) was waved to the music of drums and rattles in the Cherokee tribe's eagle dance.

Desert sport
Falconry has been popular in the Arab world for centuries. Originally, as was the case elsewhere, it was a means of catching food, such as bustards and desert hares. Now it is a popular sport.

Raptors

There are raptors on every continent except Antarctica: over 300 species of diurnal (day-flying) bird of prey and about 130 species of owl. Each of these species plays its own unique part in the ecosystem. Scientists class all the day-flying birds of prey together in the "order" (group) *falconiformes*, which contains five separate "families." The owls have their own order, the *strigiformes*.

Black vulture flying; vultures soar to look out for carrion

The king vulture; New World vultures urinate on their own legs to keep cool

Osprey

Ospreys form a one-species family. Specialists at catching fish, they eat very little else. They are found worldwide, where there are shallow waters—lakes, rivers, or coastal areas.

Pandionidae **osprey**

osprey

Secretary bird

Secretary birds are another unique species. They stand 4 ft (1.2 m) tall, and hunt by stamping on the prey they find.

Sagittariidae **secretary bird**

secretary bird

Bengal eagle owl in flight

Spectacled owl, so-called because of its facial markings

Iranian eagle owl chicks

Owls—raptors of the night

Owls are nocturnal or crepuscular (hunt at dawn and dusk). Their sight is excellent and their hearing is phenomenal. They hunt by stealth. There are two families: the dozen or so species of barn owl, and the rest.

Strigiformes **owls**

owl

New World vultures

These vultures live in the Americas, living off carrion. Although they look similar to other vultures, they are more closely related to storks, and so, according to scientific research, should no longer be classed in the *falconiformes* order. There are seven species of New World vulture.

Andean condor, largest of all raptors

The turkey vulture sniffs out its food

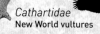

Cathartidae **New World vultures**

condor

Falcons, such as this lanner falcon, have distinctive long, pointed wings

American kestrels (right) and other kestrels are very good at hovering

Large falcons, such as this peregrine, are the fastest birds on earth when they dive

Caracaras build nests and hunt on the ground

The falconid family

There are three main groups of falcon: the true falcons, the forest falcons, and the falconets, the smallest of the raptors. The caracaras of the Americas are also related to them and form part of the *falconidae* family.

Foot of Verreaux's eagle from Africa

Large accipitrids have massively powerful feet

The African harrier hawk is halfway between a harrier and a hawk

Eagles, such as this bald eagle, can see at least twice as far as humans

Egyptian vulture shows the broad, muscular accipitrid tongue

Hooked tip of beak rips into flesh; sides of the beak cut it

Bald eagles' broad wings enable them to soar effortlessly

Accipitrids

The largest group of raptors, with 237 species. Hawks, eagles, buzzards, kites, Old World vultures, and harriers are all accipitrids. They have similar eggs, tongues, and molting patterns. They all build nests. They kill with their feet, and most have a protective ridge of bone above the eye.

Falconidae
falcons and caracaras

kestrel

Accipitridae
hawks, kites, buzzards, eagles, harriers, Old World vultures

goshawk

kite

buzzard

golden eagle

Around the world

Many of the raptors that breed in the northern hemisphere fly south for the winter (migrate). In 28 species, all the birds migrate each year. In another 42 species, the northernmost birds go south for the winter. By flying south in the fall, they avoid cold weather, short days, and less food. By going north in the spring, they can take advantage of longer days and the abundant food supplies of the northern summer. Migrating can be dangerous: hundreds of thousands of birds of prey are killed each year along migration routes.

The Philippine eagle is one of the world's largest eagles, with a particularly massive beak

Eagle in danger

The Philippine eagle is one of the rarest eagles in the world. The forests it lives in are disappearing fast. A captive breeding program is trying to restore its numbers, but unless the forest is saved, this eagle will die out in the wild.

Migrating birds cross mountain ranges by the lowest passes

More than 4 million raptors fly through Mexico each year

Migration patterns

Most raptors avoid flying over large areas of water, if possible, because it is too tiring for them. The rising air currents on which they rely do not usually occur over water. Most migrating raptors fly around seas. To move across continents, the birds all cross the shortest stretch of ocean in the region. This creates crowded flyways through which thousands of raptors pass.

The short summers of Scandinavia and other northern regions provide plenty of food for many bir[ds]

The Straits of Gibraltar is the shortest stretch of water between Europe and Africa. Nearly 800,000 raptors cross here each year.

Falsterbo

Istanbul

Cape May

Tarifa

Eilat

Panama Canal

About 1 million raptors cross between Asia and Africa over the Sinai Desert each year

Most North American raptors spend the winter in the tropics of Central and South America. Some species from the far south, such as the cinereous harrier, migrate north in autumn to escape the cold weather.

Trans-American flyway
W. European–W. African flyway
Eurasian–E. African flyway
E. Asian continental flyway
E. Asian–Oceanic flyway
Amur falcon's migratory route

Should I stay or should I go?

In some species, the birds will only move south in especially cold winters, or only move within their breeding range. This is called "partial migration." A number of species, such as buzzards (right), are partial migrants. Often, adult birds can stay farther north than juveniles, because they are better at finding food.

Tail feathers form a rounded flap that is used to slow the bird in flight

Marathon migrants

The Amur falcon has the longest migration of any raptor. It spends summer in northern China and Eastern Siberia, but flies all the way across to South Africa in winter. It flies around the Himalayas and the Arabian Sea.

Feathers on wing tips curve upward due to the force of the air pushing back during the powerful downstroke of the wings

Birds in the eastern Pacific fly from island to island as they head south

The Amur falcon's migration route has only recently been tracked. It was previously thought they flew directly over the Indian Ocean

Birds flying this route are skirting around the Himalayas, which are too high for raptors to cross

Watching Out For Raptors

From slaughter to sanctuary

Many raptors migrate across Hawk Mountain in Pennsylvania. Once, birds were shot as they flew over, but in 1934 the area was made into the world's first bird of prey sanctuary. The sanctuary organized the world's first annual hawk count and led research into raptors.

A ring for tracking a raptor

One method of finding out more about raptors is to put little metal rings on birds' legs. Birds can be ringed, and if they are trapped, or found dead, the information is sent to central collecting points. Some birds are now tracked by satellites.

Back from the brink

The California condor is the rarest bird of prey in the world. There was a dramatic fall in their numbers in the 1980s until, finally, the last wild condors were brought into captivity. Fortunately, they breed well and are now being released back into the wild.

Raptor records

The fastest bird in the world, the bird with the greatest wing area, the bird that catches the largest quarry—all these are birds of prey. In the recent past there was a species of eagle in New Zealand, Haast's eagle, that was one-third bigger than any raptor alive today. It only became extinct within the last thousand years. The actions of human beings mean many of today's most magnificent raptors may soon join it.

Largest nest

Name: Bald eagle

Record: 9½ ft (2.9 m) wide; 20 ft (6 m) deep

The largest nest built was in Florida. It was several decades old and was estimated to weigh 2 tons.

Fastest flier

Name: Gyrfalcon

Record: 68 mph (110 kph)

The largest falcon is also the fastest in horizontal flight. It lives around the edge of the Arctic.

Highest flying

Name: Rüppell's griffon vulture

Record: 37,000 ft (11,000 km)

This high-flying vulture has been seen by airliners at cruising altitude over Africa.

Fastest diver

Name: Peregrine falcon

Record: 242 mph (389 kph)

The stoop, or attacking dive, of this small falcon makes it the fastest animal on Earth, when diving.

Best hearing

Name: Barn owl

Record: Time difference: 0.00003 seconds

The barn owl can tell if a sound arrives at one ear 30 millionths of a second after it reaches the other.

Best eyesight

Name: Peregrine falcon

Record: Sees prey 1.8 miles (3 km) away

This peregrine falcon's eyesight is thought to be eight times better than that of a human.

Biggest wings

Name: Andean condor

Record: 16 sq ft (1.5 sq m)

This enormous vulture lives in the Andes mountains and can glide down to the Pacific coast to feed.

Longest migration

Name: Amur falcon

Record: 13,600 miles/22,000 km (roundtrip)

Spending summer in Manchuria and Siberia, this bird travels all the way to southern Africa in winter.

Tallest

Name: Secretary bird

Record 4 ft 4 in (1.3 m) high

This strange African raptor nests at the top of trees but hunts on foot, jumping on top of its prey.

Smallest

Name: Black thighed falconet

Record: Wingspan 11 in (27 cm)

This little raptor lives in Southeast Asia. The size of a sparrow, it feeds on insects.

Largest raptors

Swamp harrier

The swamp hawk, from New Zealand, is the largest harrier. Its wingspan is 57 in (145 cm) and it can weigh 2½ lb (1.1 kg).

Gyrfalcon

This raptor is very large for a falcon. It weighs 3 lb (1.35 kg) and has a wingspan of 51 in (130 cm). Being large helps it stay warm in its Arctic home.

Eurasian black vulture

The king vulture is the largest Old World vulture. It can weigh 24 lb (11 kg). Its wingspan is about 10 ft (3 m).

Harpy eagle

Along with the Philippines eagle, the Harpy eagle is the world's biggest eagle. It weighs 20 lb (9 kg) with a wingspan of 7 ft (2.2 m).

Great gray owl

This giant owl lives across the northern hemisphere. The females are larger than the males, with a wingspan of 56 in (142 cm) and a weight of 2¾ lb (1.25 kg).

Red kite

This widespread raptor is found across Europe, North Africa, and Western Asia. Its wingspan is 70 in (179 cm) and it weighs 2¾ lb (1.3 kg).

Ferruginous hawk

This North American hawk, which hunts in the prairies, weighs 4½ lb (2 kg) and has a wingspan of 60 in (152 cm).

Glossary

ARBOREAL
Living fully or mainly in trees.

BARB
In most feathers, the central shaft has thousands of barbs—tiny, closely spaced branches that project outward to form a continuous flat surface.

BARBULE
In a feather, a miniscule side branch that locks the barbs together, like a zipper.

BEAK
see Bill.

BILL
A bird's jaws. A bill is made of bone, with a hornlike outer coating of keratin.

Brood of one-day-old chicks

BROOD
(noun) The young birds produced from a single clutch of eggs. (verb) To sit on nestlings to keep them warm. Brooding is usually carried out mostly or entirely by the adult female.

CAMOUFLAGE
The shape or coloring of a bird that allows it to blend into its environment.

CARRION
The remains of dead animals.

CLUTCH
The group of eggs laid in a single nest, usually laid by one female and incubated together.

COLLAR
The area around the middle of a bird's neck, which in some species is a prominent feature of the plumage.

CONTOUR FEATHER
A general term for any feather that covers the outer surface of a bird, including its wing and tail. Contour feathers are also known as body feathers and help to streamline the bird.

COURTSHIP DISPLAY
Ritualized, showy behavior used in courtship by the male and sometimes by the female.

CROP
The area on top of a bird's head. It is often a distinctive plumage feature.

DIURNAL
Active during the day.

DOWN FEATHER
A soft, fluffy feather, lacking the system of barbs or contour flight feathers, that provides good insulation.

EAR TUFT
A distinct tuft of feathers on each side of the bird's forehead, with no connection to the true ears.

EGG TOOTH
A small, hornlike growth on the bill of a nestling, which it uses to break out of its shell.

FLEDGLING
A young bird that is ready to leave the nest and has acquired the first set of complete flight feathers.

FLIGHT FEATHER
A collective term for a bird's wing and tail feathers, used in flight.

FOREWING
The front section of a bird's wing, including the primary covert feathers and secondary covert feathers.

GIZZARD
A region of the bird's gut in which food is ground down before digestion.

HABITAT
The geographical and ecological area in which a particular organism usually lives.

Juvenile bateleur eagle has a brown plumage

HINDWING
The rear section of a bird's spread wing.

INCUBATE
To sit on eggs to keep them warm, allowing the embryo inside to grow. Incubation is mostly carried out by the adult female.

JUVENILE
A term referring to the plumage worn by a young bird at the time it makes its first flight and until it begins its first molt.

KEEL
Enlarged "ridge" on the breastbone that anchors the muscles that are used for flight.

KERATIN
A tough protein found in a bird's claws, feathers, and the outer part of the bill. Human hair and fingernails are also made of it.

Flight feathers of an eagle

MANTLE
The loose term used to define the back of a bird, between its neck and rump.

MIGRATION
A journey to and from different regions, following a well-defined route. Most birds that migrate regularly do so in step with the seasons.

MOLT
In birds, to shed old feathers so that they can be replaced.

NAPE
The back of the neck.

NESTLING
A young bird that is still in the nest.

NEW WORLD
The Americas, from Alaska to Cape Horn, including the Caribbean and offshore islands in the Pacific and Atlantic oceans.

NOCTURNAL
Active during the night.

OLD WORLD
Europe, Asia, Africa, and Australasia.

PREENING
Essential routine behavior of birds to keep their feathers in good condition.

PRIMARY FEATHER
One of the large outer wing feathers, growing from the digits of a bird's "hand."

QUILL
The lowest part of a feather's central shaft, which grows from the bird's skin.

ROOST
A place where birds sleep, either at night or by day.

SCRAPE
A simple nest that consists of a shallow depression in the ground, which may be unlined or lined with soft material, such as feathers and grasses.

SECONDARY FEATHER
One of the rows of long, stiff feathers along the rear edge of a bird's wing, between the body and the primary feathers at the wingtip. The secondary feathers are collectively referred to as secondaries.

SOARING
In birds, flight without flapping of the wings. On land, birds soar using rising air currents called thermals that form over warm land, or along cliffs and mountains.

SPECIES
A group of similar living things that is capable of interbreeding in the wild and of producing fertile offspring that resemble themselves. Species are often the fundamental units used in biological classification.

STERNUM
The breastbone of a vertebrate. The sternum of most birds is relatively large, with a prominent central ridge known as the keel.

Broad wings of raptors enable them to soar

STOOP
A fast, near-vertical dive made by falcons and some other birds of prey when chasing aerial prey.

TALON
The sharp, hooked claw of a bird of prey.

TARSUS
A part of the leg. In birds, it is the longest, most exposed section of the leg, between the "ankle" joint and the "toes."

Bald eagle preening its tail feathers

TEMPERATE
The regions of the world that lie at mid-latitudes, between the polar regions and the tropics and subtropics.

THERMAL
A rising bubble or column of warm air that soaring birds can make use of to gain height with little effort. Thermals only occur over land.

UNDERWING
The underside of the wing.

UPPERWING
The top side of the wing.

VANE
In most feathers, the flat surface on either side of the central shaft. The vane is largest in wing feathers.

VENT
The area of feathers between the base of the bird's tail and its legs.

WINGSPAN
The distance across a bird's outstretched wings and back, from one wingtip to another.

Talons of an eagle

Index

Acknowledgments

Dorling Kindersley would like to thank:
Everyone at the National Birds of Prey Centre, near Newent, Gloucestershire, England (Craig Astbury, John Crooks, Monica Garner, Ian Gibbons, Debbie Grant, Breeze Hale, Angie Hill, Philip Jones, Kirsty Large, Mark Parker, Mark Rich, Jan Stringer). The Booth Natural History Museum, Brighton (Jeremy Adams); Dr Steve Parry. Sean Stancioff for research and editorial assistance. Julie Ferris and Iain Morris for design assistance; Bill Le Fever, Gilly Newman, and John Woodcock for artwork; Iain Morris for Endpapers; Marion Dent for Indexing; Steve Gorton, Alex Wilson, and C Laubscher for additional photography; Tom Jackson for additional textl; and Chris Hawkes for text editing.

The publisher would like to thank the following for their kind permission to reproduce the images:

Picture credits: t=top, b=bottom, c=center, l=left, r=right

123RF.com: Dennis Van De Water 36c, Lynn Bystrom 71tr, 71cb, Matyas Rehak 69cla, Miroslav Liska 32bl, Nico Smit 70, Steve Byland 69cra. **Alamy Images:** AfriPics.com 32tr, Danita Delimont Creative 69tc, Dave Watts 44–45b, 45clb, FLPA 40cl, 69bl, Ian Wray 37tc, Johnny Jones 61bc, RM Asia 49c, Simon Balson 41tr. **Ardea, London:** Eric Dragesco 20tl. **British Museum:** Front Cover tl, Back Cover tl, 58tr, 62tr/63tl. **Bruce Coleman Collection:** Jane Burton 57bl, Raimund Cramm 38bl, Peter Davey 68c, Francisco J. Erize 8bc, Pekka Helo 47tr, Gordon Langsbury 34tl, Mary Plage 23tl, Marie Read 50crb, N. Schwiatz 30cl, Uwe Walz 46br, Joseph Van Warmer 47br, Staffan Widstrand 12br, Rod Williams 9tl. **Corbis:** Alan Murphy / BIA / Minden Pictures 60, Alexander Koenders / Nature in Stock 36b, Ch'ien

Lee / Minden Pictures 45tr, cultura 60–61, Eric and David Hosking 55tr, Markus Varesvuo / Nature Picture Library 44tl, Martin Willis / Minden Pictures 40cra, Oscar Diez / BIA / Minden Pictures 40cla, Ron Austing / FLPA 54bc, Sean Crane / Minden Pictures 40–41, Wim Werrelman / NIS / Minden Pictures 69bc. **Cornell Laboratory of Ornithology, New York:** L. Page Brown 38tl. **Dorling Kindersley:** British Wildlife Centre, Surrey, UK 68bl, Cotswold Wildlife Park 69cr, E. J. Peiker 69br, Liberty's Owl, Raptor and Reptile Centre, Hampshire, UK 36tc, 49tr, 68bc, 71br, Natural History Museum, London 61tc, 70cl. **Dreamstime. com:** Amreshm 48–49t, Blossfeldia 33br, Brian Kushner 68cra, Dbtale 55b, Eduard Kyslynskyy 32–33b, Edward Hu 67tl, 69tl, jose 37tl, Isselee 69ca, Jamesvancouver 68tr, Jose Antonio Nicoli 69cc, Musat Christian 32–33c, Niek 45br, Paul Reeves 68cla, Rafael Arroyo Argudo 48–49b, Sergei Zlatkov 67tr; **Dover Publications:** 64cra, 9cla, 28tl, 30c, 68tl. **Mary Evans Picture Library:** 42cl, 46tl, 47cl, 51tr, 52tr, 63br, Back cover cr. **Frank Lane Picture Agency:** John Hawkins 47cr, Alan Parker 53tr. **Giraudon, Paris:** 23cb, Avec Authorisation speciale de la Ville De Bayeux 62bl, 62tl. **Robert Harding Picture**

Library: Photri inc. 34cr. Hawk Mountain Sanctuary Association, PA, USA: Wendy Scott 67cr. **iStockphoto.com:** drferry 40b; naturepl.com: Andy Trowbridge 54–55, Eric Baccega 36–37, Roger Powell 41br; **Science Photo Library:** Duncan Shaw 54l, Jaime Chirinos 48bl, Linda Wright 55tl, 61crb. Peter Newark's Pictures: 46clb. **NHPA:** Alan Williams 68cr. **Jemima Parry-Jones:** 65tl, 38bc, 42tl, 51crb, 68br, Miguel Lopez 43tl. **Planet Earth:** D. Robert Franz 35tl, Nick Garbutt 53cla, William S. Paton 53tl, David A Ponton 64cl, Mike Read 57tr, Ronald S.Rogoff 47tc, Johnathan Scott 50tc, 50cl, Anup Shah 68cl. **Kati Poynor:** 31tl. **RSPB:** M. W. Richards 34bl. **Frank Spooner Pictures:** Gamma/F. Soir 67cb. **Micheal Zabé:** 63tc. **Wild Wonders of Europe:** 33t

All other images © Dorling Kindersley
For further information see: www.dkimages.com